This Many Miles from Desire

This Many Miles from Desire

Poems by Lee Herrick

WordTech Editions

For Luis,

Hope you enjoy the book. Your art is breathtaking —

Peace & blessings,

Lee Herrick

11/08

Published by WordTech Editions
P.O. Box 541106
Cincinnati, OH 45254-1106

Typeset in Perpetua by WordTech Communications LLC,
Cincinnati, OH

ISBN: 9781933456614
LCCN: 2007922304

Poetry Editor: Kevin Walzer
Business Editor: Lori Jareo

Cover and author photo: Polly A. Begley

Visit us on the web at www.wordtechweb.com

The author would like to express his gratitude to the editors of the following publications, where some of the poems in this collection previously appeared:

Berkeley Poetry Review: "Georgia"
Haight Ashbury Literary Journal: "Backs," "Crossword," "Dreamer," "What Is Sacred"
Hawai'i Pacific Review: "Lines"
Hurricane Blues: Poems About Katrina and Rita: "A Thousand Saxophones"
inside english: "Gravity"
Korean Quarterly: "The Violinst"
Many Mountains Moving: "Three Dreams of Korea: Notes on Adoption"
MiPOesias: "Korean Adoptee Returns to Seoul," "Korean Adoptee Daydreams"
Penumbra: "Raison D'etre"
Peralta Press: "Ars Poetica"
Quercus Review: "Four Types of Jeong"
Willow Review: "Adoption Music"

These poems appeared in a chapbook of poems, *Coping With Vertigo*, published by Talent House Press:

"Air," "Belief," "For Andres and Eleanor," "Slowness," "Yoga on the Beach"

For Polly

with love to my mother, father, and sister

Contents

1.

To suffer is not enough. We must also be in touch with the wonders of life.

Thich Nhat Hanh

Ars Poetica

Yes, the ocean is Buddhist. And the foam
scrambling onto the beach is a symphony
of cymbals, small and caring like mothers
whispering to their children in the front pew,
sssshhh. Perhaps then the trees should
believe in God. Of course. How they reach
straight up after all those years like the Chinese
grandmothers rising at dawn, when the air's
cleanest, an orchestra of their own, stretching
toward the sun. None of this true. The ocean
is only Buddhist because a poet writes of it
that way—just like the grandmothers who keep
surfacing in his poems, usually dancing
somewhere near a body of water, blissfully.

Adoption Music

I am learning to play the taiko, to feel
how leaves reappear in the trees with such ease.
One monk says this will teach me to hear
the variations of my name:
how my lover sighs it,
how a teacher grinded it out like a curse,
how your mother says it, drowning in a lake
before she leaves you. How it means somewhere
between mothers, not quite the rose
but not quite the roots. Like the woman
who finds you says, *Lee*, like a discovery—
one more child found in the world's history
of found children. How she said it like the echo
of one plucked e string, a clear pang of delight.

Hands

They imagine the lines of their palms like maps of a city.
At night they like to align them, clasping each other's futures gently.

Tonight they stare at those shapes, the hope and intrigue
of their various constellations.

And he imagines her hand as one, a fusion
of water, bone, light.

He imagines it the center of their own starry arrangement,
that dream about serenity they discuss each year.

And their hands callous from the work of it,
the labor of curiosity, asking the hands why

the skin rises toward God through work.

Tonight, they examine the texture of their hands
and take new vows. To rub the palm gently more often.

To work at defining the sky. To care for each other's hands
like small children, recently born into the world.

Gravity

A partially deflated balloon landed
in our backyard, the evidence of some

young boy's experiment that proves
gravity is a fact, that what is released

must come down, like when his mother
let go of the boy's father. Like a balloon

he floated off into the horizon until
he disappeared beyond the trees, and

somewhere, perhaps in the Midwest or Texas,
he has landed in another child's life.

This is when the boy starts to believe
in what he cannot see, like faith and God,

but even though his mother says it exists,
he doesn't quite believe in love.

Gravity means someone will receive the love.
It's not all that much work to love,

his mother says. Listen for the opportunity
and run alongside it, let your hair blaze

through the wind. Let everything go
if the wind decides to take control.

The angels orchestrate it all, anyway.
They have landed on a cloud on tested

all the theories--relativity, evolution, keeping
all the answers to themselves. In a moment

of levity the boy begins to love his mother
because she can hold a handful of balloons

and let them all go free, let them all slither
up into the sky like little air-packed circles

of guilt. He imagines her smiling
at the mirror for the first time in years,

like she used to do before
the father floated away.

In the evenings, when he imagines clouds
landing on the ground like tumbleweeds

in the middle lane, he is certain that gravity
will rule the day and that all those words

he has lofted into the air—hope and love
and a woman's name he will someday marry—

will land in someone's backyard and inspire
something kind, something extraordinary,

like a soft tiny cloud, landing
in the palm of your hand.

Crossword

I can still hear my mother saying *patience*
after waiting for the word to arrive
from the clue, *a virtuous quality*—
there was always sunlight streaming
into the kitchen, tea steaming

At ten, I liked the impermanence of pencil
so I could erase the answers I thought to be true.
So my favorite six letter words used to imply
a tenuous existence like *mirage, affair, cobweb.*

Now, twenty years later
I have unlearned all those words (except for patience)
and I prefer choose a more permanent vocabulary:
words like *faith, smile, adopt.*

My favorite word, Eugene O'Neill's
_____ Under the Elms (six letters)
is synonymous with love, war, future

I have learned a tabby is a female domestic cat
and conbrio means with musical vigor,
and that no human emotion is black and white—
colors reserved for piano keys or tuxedos.
Even crossword puzzles in the Sunday
Times are mirages down a long, winding road,
stars emerging for the night,
you behind the wheel, dreaming

of all the beautiful words you can _____.
(Lennon tune, seven letters)

Three Dreams of Korea: Notes on Adoption

1.

This one happens in morning
as a nearby crow wakes me,
calling *God, God, look at this* :
I am on the steps of a church,
wrapped in Monday's *Korea Times*
telling of the drought in Pusan.
You can live by the water
and still die of thirst, and I,
there on the cold brick steps,
am dying. But dying
means the presence of breath.
This one happens on Hangul Day,
Independence Day in Seoul,
where girls in purple satin
hanboks parade through
downtown streets. In this dream
I make eye contact with
every single one of them.
Another boy, a few years
older than I, rides
a tricycle in the parade,
trailing the girls.
He sees me. He winks,
as if he knows how
everything will end.

2.

This one happens in the evening
just as daylight surrenders to the moon,
and the flute of dusk arrives.
It is cool.
I am wrapped in a sky blue blanket,
so whoever finds me thinks kindly
of whoever left me.
The one who finds me is a nun.
She opens the door, looking
beyond me
into the tired night,
then looks down.
She gasps softly.
She says, *ahneyong*, you sweet
beautiful child. She bends
down like an angel
and takes me
into her arms.

3.

This one happens in the cruelest moment
of the day, as heat curls flowers
into dirt. A man, drunk
with despair, screams at the sun.
His sorrow is a collage of
moths and ants, crawling
from his face to his chest.
I watch from the steps.
It is the year of the dog
and I am a part of it :
unable to speak

but an expert at listening :
to the old man from Laos who sits
on the steps two buildings down :
he is telling another man
how Hmong children become human
on the third day of life,
after the soul calling ceremony
and the burning of animal flesh.
He smokes from a pipe
and closes his eyes as he inhales.
I can hear all of this.
I can hear a woman rustling inside the church.
She is a dancer, so she speaks with her hands.
I hear her rise, sweetly
from her knees to her feet.
This means she believes
in dreams. I hear her
slide her hand, sweetly
along her hair. This means
she believes in the sun.
I hear her move towards me
and place her open palm on the door.
This means she welcomes me.
This means she believes
in the miracle of possibility.

Lines

I only saw two in Beijing—not at any restaurant,
where you lean in and jockey for position against the hordes

or just let the food arrive when it will. Not at the international
airport where the same rules apply. But in the evening

when the thirty grandmothers came out to dance in lines
their arms curling like thin flags around their bodies.

They formed a square, really, a gathering of years
stepping softly in perfect time to the music.

The other one was a true line, hundreds of tourists long,
entering Chairman Mao's Mausoleum. It was official business

armed guards politely taking our cameras, backpacks,
bottles of water, saying *you can get this when you are through*

the line. We filed in one by one, walking swiftly
up to the body encased in glass, his belly rising under the flowers,

an occasional tourist from Shanghai or Denver trying
to slow down, to better capture this moment, the guards

nudging them along saying, *keep this line moving*—
And then there are the ones I remember from school

The dreadful kickball line, up against the wall so the strong kids
could decide who to pick, who to pick, eyeing each scrawny kid

to fill out their team, each of us looking down at the sad gravel
wishing we could burrow into it and out of this lineup—

And now there are the ones I think about most, the lonely couplet,
the boastful quatrain, the curving lineage of my father's and mother's

pasts, the unfinished one of my future, and mostly these new ones,
these slight mirages that appear when I look in the mirror and smile,

the stories written right there beside my eyes, almost like the thirty
grandmothers, these fables dancing among us.

Backs

There are thousands and thousands of steps,
each one a perfectly leveled plate of stone,
on the way to the top of Tai Shan.
As with all five sacred mountains in China,
a story surrounds it like a shawl, shared
with travelers like me whose awe is measurable
by the breath it takes to honor them by climbing.
I take the seven hour day as it comes to me, resting
for water when my body wants to surrender
amidst the other sojourners with sweaty backs,
some with gore-tex packs loaded with energy
bars and maps, most with backs like mine
arched from fatigue.

At the top of Tai Shan you witness,
in all your clear exhaustion, what the backs
of men and women created—a city seven hours
closer to heaven. They stretched thick wooden
poles across their backs and balanced, huge
buckets on each end, carrying what they could—
unbreakables at the bottom: tools, cloth, plastics—
tender necessities at the top: eggs, plates, glass.

Last summer I saw one man going up
as I went down in the mechanical lift.
The pole bowed at the ends like a gradual frown
from the buckets' weight. He was no more
than five feet tall with muscles like planets,
bulging and floating around the sun of his body,

his biceps like fists.

His muscular back must have been what
the old men in Korea used to boast before
their lives became days full of shuffling
to the neighborhood card game. Their sloped
backs are like mine, resembling nothing
of their grandson's muscular ones,
straight and carved, appropriate for their
military hats. Their young backs are smooth—

the product of Nautilus machines in air
conditioned gyms, but still foundation enough,
bridges that will carry parents in the difficult
hours of their lives to the soft
places they have worked to earn.

Korean Adoptee Returns to Seoul

How can I tell you that my wife and I slept
behind three temples and some vendors flapping
the *Korea Times* at the flies on the durian

that in this racing city, the sleek Lexus races
down fast lanes, past skyrise malls

and sidewalk food stalls while the old men
call it a day and do not notice me at all,

a Korean adoptee smelling Seoul
for the first time in the thirty years?

The first night back, I dream about birth
rights and death dates, birthdates and love
lost somewhere over the Pacific.

The first night back, I dream in that hotel room
behind the temples about a birth scenario.

I dream about the woman whose body bore me,
right here in this city thirty years ago, where

that same vendor flapped the newspaper
at the flies on the durian, eighteen years after
the Korean War when Russians took the north

Americans took the south, below the thin line
that served as the new border. Maybe

she was thirty and I took too much from her
busy life and she could not imagine death

so she left me on the steps of a church.
Maybe she was sixteen, and

I was heavy on her heart and on her back
so heavy that in her dreams, I could sink
quietly, in a lake.

Have I mentioned this to you?
Have I mentioned how downtown Seoul

collides with the horizon, how I could smell
pieces of Fresno even here at the barbecued squid

vendor's five foot business, how close Pyongyang
feels when I am in Fresno among the blossoms,

the cement, and the hopeful ones like me and you,
counting on tomorrow being good?
Have I mentioned how Seoul is a city

in which I have loved and been loved, left and been
left, a city in which I found green plants raging

out of the earth, trees reaching toward the sun
with such vertical precision you'd think God,

yes, God had been involved in the planting?
I should mention how the sun tries to blaze there

like the sun tries to blaze here, how the son

finally rests having been home and smelled the city
and its possessions: the garlic fields, the rice fields,

and the woman's hands mixing
the kimchi into the egg

How his heartbeat sounds as if it is saying *life*
life   life   life   deep like the water

that connects these two cities
and the light breeze that blows in between.

Four Types of Jeong

There are four types of Korean jeong (similar to the Western
conception of love): that expressed between mother and son,
between friends, between lovers, and for universal compassion.

1.

Last night, the smell of wild jasmine
flowers perfumed my dream. On the beach,

three hundred miles from here, a mother
held her young son's hands as the ends of the waves

licked at his feet. She named him after a famous painter,
so his life beyond her might find a yellow light

in the black moonless hours of night.

2.

One boy pretends he's Bruce Lee. Carving the air,
his friend pretends to be Jet Li. They make a pact

to be like brothers no matter where their fathers go,
no matter how the angels sing for them.

When one calls out for the other, moaning
into the vacant city in a time of need, he drops

everything and runs to him as fast as he possibly can.

3.

A man walks with a woman, hands lightly clasped.
He rubs his finger along the back of her hand.

This was *palja*, fate, written in the histories centuries ago
that they would laugh like this, on this beach.

This is his heart on a wire, electric and exposed
and glorious in its circumstance.

This is his language, dancing in time with hers.

4.

The last love is like the moon, the sun, and the air.
It encompasses what you cannot name, the mothers

and sons on the verge of dissolution, the boyhood
friends separated by war, and the lovers who hearts

go blind from fatigue. This love is for a man gone mad,
hunched in a damp cell twenty two hours a day,

dreaming of what it felt like to be touched.

Vision as Delicacy

A tender balance—the glassy lens of your eye
against what we endure: the allergic explosion

swelling the lids, the unfiltered sun on the river—

Often, the eye becomes a delicacy—the man of honor
eating the fish eye in east China, how the eye watches him,

hopes for him, even in its fleshy socket.

In the marketplace, that eye on the side of the dead pig's head,
white and round and ready for the fire,

reminds a man of the delicate nature of love,
the circular nature of vision at its best,

a fusion of death and light. Close both
eyes softly. Notice the weight of the lids,

the heightened sense of your own miraculous breath

making its way out. How startling to
open your eyes and take the world in,

one amazing vision at a time.

Korean Adoptee Daydreams

A slow bow screeched against the E
and you were so beautiful. Somewhere

my birth mother finds God and music
she knows will be her saving moment's

backdrop: a brave hue like the sun,
a bright light like her son

reading Eliot in California with a wife.

We should be so lucky to have these days
whose leaves bend right

on warm nights. Yes, let the good earth calm
this morning here in Korea, guns and black

hair waving in the easy wind, a father
who has finally forgotten everything.

Across the Pacific in Holland and America
we have been properly Westernized, lamenting

we never had rice with each meal or
a kisongbok made for our special day.

We master the art called dreaming.
I could teach you the history of dreams

and lamenting. Yes, a lament is a violin bow
that must go back and forth, best

accompanied by a clean piano, a clean window,
and a view of the sea of your choice.

Korean Adoptee in Phnom Penh

I saw a mother whistle at her son
as he pedaled out into a field.
He froze.
She learned to teach
freezing because her brothers
use a wooden cane, one leg blown
to hell by the little mines
designed to mame, not kill.

She wants to live and let
her son live life
loaded with good food and good luck
so she keeps one eye on him as he plays.
The other eye is for me.

Here, tonight, on the main road
back from the river,
I hold my wife's tender hand,
our legs in sync like a dream,
both of us praying
in the half calm
Phnom Penh
night

Salvation

The blues is what mothers do not tell their sons,
in church or otherwise, how their bodies forgave
them when their spirits gave in, how you salvage love
by praying for something acoustic, something clean

and simple like the ideal room, one with a shelf
with your three favorite books and a photo
from your childhood, the one of you with the
big grin before you knew about the blues.

I wonder what songs my birth mother sang in
the five months she fed me before she left me
on the steps of a church in South Korea.
I wonder if they sounded like Sarah Chang's

quivering bow, that deep chant of a mother
saying goodbye to her son. Who can really say?
Sometimes all we have is the blues. The blues means
finding a song in the abandonment, one

you can sing in the middle of the night when
you remember that your Korean name, Kwang Soo
Lee, means bright light, something that can illuminate
or shine, like tears, little drops of liquefied God,

glistening down your brown face. I wonder
what songs my birth mother sings and if she sings
them for me, what stories her body might tell.
I have come to believe that the blues is the body's

salvation, a chorus of scars to remind you
that you are here, not where you feared you would be,
but here, flawed, angelic, and full of light.
I believe that the blues is the spirit's wreckage,

examined and damaged but whole again, more full
and prepared than it's ever been, quiet and still,
just as it was always meant to be.

2.

You are the music while the music lasts.

T. S. Eliot

Raison D'etre

after Collins

This is the beginning. Almost anything can happen.
On stage, the house lights dim and a curtain rises.
The first tomato of the year. A boom of thunder.
This is where you realize you are falling in love.
This is January, the green digital clock beeping
you into Monday At 6:00 a.m., 6:00 a.m., 6:00 a.m.
This is the first time you saw her and the last time
you saw her. This is first guitar chord of the opening
song on the first date of a month long tour.
The cool sand on a clean beach. This is where
you learn how to ask questions
in order to get what you want.

This is the middle. The stomach moaning for lunch,
a child with bloody elbows, a thrown stone beginning
its descent. This is the turning point of the film
where you think, *this is starting to get good.*
This is the gas station bathroom on a five hour drive.
This is the bridge, the refrain, the leap from a perfectly
Good plane. This is the batch of tomatoes that becomes
a gift for a friend. Here is a time to think, *my God
What have I done?* Make your substitutions.
Get the right players on the field.
This is the apology, suspended
in midair like a cloud.

And this, this is the end. This is the guitarist
smashing the amp, the last lip of the sun over the hills.

Here we discover our reason for being, the black mascara
on a widow's cheek, and the solemn bow to the crowd.
Here is the moon, December, midnight. This is Friday,
the exhale after too long a wait. This is the coda,
the swan howling at the lake, a moon bloated
with deathbed prayers. This is like a beginning.
A circle of sorts. Here is where you realize love
assumes the shapes of flowers in damp backyards,
denying the temptation to wilt.

How to Spend a Birthday

Light a match. Watch the blue part

                    flare like a shocked piñata

              from the beating
              into the sky,

                  watch how fast thin

wood burns & turns toward the skin,

the olive-orange skin of your thumb

                        & let *it* burn, too.

Light a fire. Drown out the singing cats.

Let the drunken mariachis blaze their way,

streaking like crazed hyenas

over a brown hill, just underneath

a perfect birthday moon.

Dancing Near a Body of Water

You are the heart and the lungs of this ocean
by which I wave my earthly body, my simple arms
curling like commas into the foam. Yes,
you are the heart and the lungs of this ocean

because we agree to let it be this way tonight,
your smile the way home, our home nowhere near.
In Panajel, I would dance by the drums and scream
in Spanish about love and miracles.

In Qingdao, I would pray by the Yellow Sea for our
good return and luck and health for our parents.
In Lima, I would dance above the crashing waves
and think about valor and family.

In Hue, at night on the coast, there are no bullets
tonight. I would dance to save our lives.
Yes, I would dance for you until there was no
more rhythm to the world, until the all the drums

lost their skins and the birds forgot how to fly.
I would dance for you here in this living room
with our cats nodding in approval, or in that
room in Cusco where we slept together under

the alpaca blanket. That night, I dreamed I was
the ocean. Yes, I was the body of water,
you were the heart and the lungs.

Breathing

Easiest in the evening—those cool jaunts
to the lake, a fire waltzing in the place

where you proposed on one knee with a single flower
for a reason to water that garden each day.

And how soon we forget what luscious
bulbs lie beneath the dirt, bellowing

up like a final moan of ecstasy, a gasp of unusual
bliss. Occasionally though—just occasionally

enough to hear the breath of a cat, we capture
the life and death of it, the long and short

answers those children hamper us over—no
ordinary secret that bulbs prefer jazz in June,

no ordinary emotion, April's giddiness—

the sound of one deep breath and the slow
release of it back into the void.

Beauty (My Plain Idea)

Is the dirt you shake from the root—
not the part closest to heaven (the petal),

not even the aphids having their way.
Beauty is forgetting how

the root hangs on but the dirt lets go.

Tonight, I dream about water: drowning in it,
floating on it, the particles we cannot see:

all the body's water keeping us alive,
the ghosts in every room.

Tonight, I weigh their echoes.
I wonder if good fortune means a bird

who remembers you, a ghost in the room approving
the lines you write, how your birth was a death

nearly delivered, how you recover and
become a believer. The blooming flowers around

you have all the answers. Be quiet. You should

hear them aspiring under this very floor.

Korean Adoptee Thinks about Plants

I should chronicle——plants
roots or the air
       yes, maybe

it's the air that should rule
the day, how elusive it is
how it equalizes and delivers

the minimum wage thief
from the CEO felon

But the plants want love, too——
they lean into the sun like children diving
      off the board saying *watch me,*

watch me, but it's mostly just the sun
watching, the air caring
about the browning leaves before you
come and snip them

And the roots——I should insert
easy metaphor about my own
deep ones or lack of them
      born, loved, left,

found, chosen, loved again and again,
these roots digging into
the earth like an apology

The Violinst

after Stephen Wunrow's photograph of Sarah Chang,
Asian-American violinist

Sarah, I've every desire to feel your hands
and come to the ancient conversation between you
and Max Bruch there, steady on the bow.
Here is the definition of softness, the way you hold
the neck just as you did when you were eight
for the New York Philharmonic.
If you let go, would the music float to heaven?
Or would it flutter around my ear, brushing
itself against me like a child?
Sarah, if I had an hour with you
I would pray for the notes
we have the fortune to absorb
and let them stand
for the one hundred ways
I imagine your smile, curling at the end
of the concerto, blowing the roof into the sky.

Listening to Janis Joplin

My arm on the sill, where a fly carves
its space in dust. There is nothing outside today.
Inside, bowls go ignored and harden
for the coming summer. The fire grows old in the bricks.
Joan told me once how Janis died but I can't recall it now.
I place the needle on the record and watch
her voice scratch up and out through the window,
fluttering like a moth gone mad. It hovers by the lightbulb
by which I've defined this year, twenty nine to the day
since Janis went out and never came back.
How did that story go, Joan?
I thought whiskey was involved, wasn't it?
Nothing violent, though—just excess.
And who said excess is a crime?
It's all there in "Crybaby," but you have to prepare
to receive. So I scrub those incessant bowls in the sink,
light a candle and watch the smoke
surrender to the wind. The fire has expired.
The moon is full.
And I still haven't figured it out.

For Bob Marley

It's a strange courage/you give me, ancient star.

--Wallace Stevens, "Nuances of a Theme By William

On a beach south of Santa Barbara—late teens
I discovered you and the difficulty of coming back from madness.

I sat alone on the beach. As surfers climbed home

and children's sandcastles surrendered to the ocean,
I pulled on my headphones and slipped

into the courage and starlight of *Is This Love?*
It reminded me of Korea and the spare clarity of a plucked string.

I sat there under a canopy of constellations
with the memory of music in Seoul—

my feet curled into the sand, and you
chanting, *could you be, could you be, could be loved ?*

I thought I warranted some love. I still do.

Maybe I was saved that night
by a God with some time on his hands

and your wailing voice, mixed with the light of the moon.

Dreamer (on the Impossibility of Driving through a Rainbow)

Tonight, I want to be the boy
who used to think he was Billy Joel
not because 1978 was anything
but a year of disco and big hair
but because it reminds me I used to dream

squinting into the stage lights waving
to the fans in the cheap seats
because they were my fans too
like the ones who paid
top dollar for the front-row
clarity of the *Piano Man*'s keys

In my yellow room at the end of the hall,
I became a legend
swirling my hips like Bob Marley
and it didn't matter that at night
I scrubbed with all my little strength
for that washcloth to turn my skin white

because when the audience roared
I sang like a God might sing
or like a man who still knows how to dream.
But how to do it now, two decades older
in a life of alarm clocks, bills stacked
near dishes crusting in the sink?

Try this: lose your clothes, be horribly late

to something and let it be that way.

Tonight, count the stars or imagine yourself
walking through a rainbow's conclusion
and remember that dreaming means tasting
all seven colors of it at once, the purple
like a brash cabernet, the red like watermelon
in June, and so on, and so on. Remember that

dreaming is survival: the willingness

to push the front door open,
set the bass just how you like it,
turn the volume up through the roof,
and sing like your throat was on fire.

Like You Were the Only Man

after Janis Joplin

At the plunk of a quarter, her voice is
like a slow river rising, deep as a well.

There should be a compass at the start
to find one's way. Without it,

she is likely to forget you, to lose you
in a sad song of wailing thick water

stories hinged on an elbow at the bar's
dusty wall, eyes looking out past dusty cars,

past Douglass Boulevard, into the orchard
where she could swear dreams run to die.

Life is Good (April At Rincon)

The heart can only send (pump) the blood so far
before it returns, recircs:

cut your losses, put on some Zeppelin,
put the needle on the record and breathe

stretch and breathe, water the plants
before they make a spectacle of you,

all your dying plants, your one cactus.

Will the music play for you when you need it?
Will you dance like no one is watching?

      There are purple flowers in the green ice plant.
      My wife reads next to me and laughs out loud.

      These waves. These perfect minutes.

You were right.

Evening in December

No sound. None. Except the tap
from the cat's four paws. Now a few rain drops

like a drummer boy learning jazz, slapping
on roof. The scrape of the match on the box.

A full flash of flame and sizzle on the kindling.
Smoke hisses out of the bricks.

Now a piece of dry wood cracks, a cymbal
to go with the rain outside. It has become

an orchestra of natural sounds, all these reasons
to believe in God surrounding us, waiting

for the seasons to change us into something good,
something in which others can believe,

like the foundations of a mother's enduring love,
the dust from across 99 blowing east.

Here, let me say, I am home: near fire,
near water, near songs of the natural world.

Belief

I go around believing everything. I believe that
the leaves turn orange in October out of fatigue.
I believe that an acoustic can heal.
I believe just a little in all of your Gods
and even more in the compassion with which you
praise them. I believe what Nietzsche said, that
without music, life would be a mistake.
I believe in my own mistakes and deities.
The way they gather around me at night
like feeding birds. I believe in the sound of my breath.
I have discovered the pleasure of belief, the surrender
of the intellectual, and the moment when thought
gives way to the heart. I believe what Paz said, that
the many who read poems worm their way into
immeasurable realities, and in the mirror of words,
discover their own infinity. I believe in manifestos.
I believe in collecting and keeping and giving back.
I believe in the day I gathered fifteen petals of a fallen
pink rose, and let them stand for my failures and
aspirations. I believe in the strength of a tired
mother, reading poems in secrecy,
discovering the sound of her voice.

A Thousand Saxophones

After Hurricane Katrina—A Poem for the Living and the Dead

You can live by the water and still die of thirst.
I said you can live by the water and still die of thirst
or the worst nightmare come true:
that body of water taking over the bodies.
Sometime, tonight, see which echoes most—
a whisper or a scream. Make it something beautiful,
like, *we will endure* or *Yes, I love you.* Sometime,
tonight, think of water—how it purifies or terrifies,
cleanses, gives and takes away—think how fast
some things can rise—water, fear, the intensity of a prayer.
Officials in New Orleans said they want to save the living.
I hope they do. But I hope they can also honor the dead.
On Bourbon Street, there were over 3,000 musicians employed
on any given day. Last night, before I fell asleep,
I imagined what a thousand saxophones
would sound like if they all played together—
one thousand saxophones, different songs,
different tempos, Dixieland, Miles Davis.
Maybe it would sound like birds or bombs,
planes or preachers praising the Word
on a hot Sunday and the congregation saying *Amen*,
some people whispering it, some people screaming it.
Maybe it would sound like lightning tearing
open the sky or a thousand books slammed shut after
a horrible conclusion, or a thousand children crying for their
mothers or fathers. Last night, I thought, how far
would a thousand saxophones echo from New Orleans or Biloxi?

Would we hear them in Fresno? Could we imagine the sound?
Could Baton Rouge? Could Washington D.C.?
I don't know what I should tell you.
But I feel like the saints are marching.
They are singing a slow, deep, and beautiful song,
waiting for us to join in.

3.

Enjoy yourself. It's later than you think.

Chinese Proverb

Yoga on the Beach

When surfers depart & the sun gives way
To the moon, it is holy. Occasional seagulls.
A sleek seal watches. Tenderly
With eyes closed, a woman with no clothes
Suspends the air with her finest act of balance
To date. When everything falls away
See how she gathers the birds. See how
She gathers their sweetness. On the tongue.
With the skin. See how she carves in the sand,
This is where everything begins.

In the Tower District, Fresno

There are fragments
of everything. An artist draws

the sun on the verge of arrival.
Andres the poet says you can't fight

this heat, it's too large for us,
so pleasure must be discovered

in the submission. Two boys walk,
one in front of the other, holding him

by a leash. A Chihuahua smiles
at the basil from Piemonte's, approves

and nods at the smokers
in front of the Revue. A Mexican

boy rides a low-rider bicycle slowly.
As his feet complete a rotation—

Coolio finishes a verse.
No one sweats here,

where small dogs rule
and a young woman

with swirling tattoos excavates
her lover's mouth,

her tongue stud sparkling
from the sinking sun.

Slowness

A man peddles flowers from his cart--his face
a potato baking in Iowa heat. His post lunch
ribusto winds a chianti song & dissolves into air.
A brunette with *Infinite Jest*
clutched at her breast. Like a tongue
waltzes to a Coltrane sax.
A cab driver dreams of sleep, sex,
fluid. He is armed with a screenplay plot
& 8 tracks of Helfgott or Bach.
On this street, a perfectly parked car is
the cup's last piece of ice, refusing
the smack of your hand.

Air

Musk dust of a hundred year room
frames European students. Sweaty
olive jasmine on a Korean woman's wrist.
She holds an African coffee.
The steam spirals businessman too busy for soap.
Watch how the clean ones sniff at their pits
to confirm the Camels didn't seep,
the Old Spice endured.
Watch how she sighs creamed coffee,
fusili and mushroom leftovers,
sewing her own stitch
into the macrame air.

Lessons

Mom taught me to say *thank you*
to total strangers because no one
is a total stranger, no one can totally be
anything. She taught that gratitude
is a star you spin in the world you make,
a shelf where nothing bad can fall.
Dad taught me what silence evokes
when the light comes into the room
at dawn. It means history has arrived
and we should excel in our desire
to live, nothing more but the desire
to work toward something tangible,
a smile on a child's face, a watercolor
of a Greek dancer, swirling her sash
like she was taught.

Father's Voice

What goes blank in the child's mind
when the sound of the father's voice
cannot be heard or even conceived?
Would it be soft? Would it be deep
enough to make you swoon? Perhaps
the sound of a father's voice is like a
flower, opening and shrinking at the
weather's discretion, the light a woman
might provide or take away. How
much light does a child need to grow
into something worth saving, worth
recollecting in a tranquil field, gold
stalks of corn and whole miles swaying
back into the earth, like a whisper.

Georgia

She's never heard the words
he looks just like you
but those who know us
say we're just like mother and son.
She paints miracles with water
and kept me.

In the Asia Market on Shaw Avenue
Ha sells me jars of kimchi
and invites me to her church.
One day, I will go.

I'll go the country
where I was born and left,
found by a nun
across the Yellow Sea,
Yantai to the west,
Sado east.

I will go and learn
the art of balance
on the famous parallel, where
fifteen year old boys
hold new guns
and practice
the warrior look.

Here in this country I devour
the commonalities

like news, baseball, gardening.

It's ten thousand miles
from Fresno
to Seoul. I'll go soon.
Along the way

lessons surrender to hours.
Women's faces appear
and disappear.

Yours,
like always,
remains.

Ode to the Graduate

(For Op: What I Keep Thinking About As You Receive Your Master's Degree)

Mostly, it's music and nature and God:
you, my dreaming brother, one of his finest children

working it out, a tongue on fire,
an angel on the ninth cloud,

deserving as a body of light. You,
my friend, on such an occasion—

you are beautiful at emerging.
Look how you shine.

Look how life is the flawed but
perfect chord. Look how you are loved.

I keep thinking about how fiercely
you have arrived and how beautifully

you have always been here—a brother
I would have chosen, even had I never

left Korea. I am never far
from you, Op. I am learning

about friendship and strength.
Can you hear me?

Can you hear me
pray you remember the steps: how each day

is a gift and that you give gifts twice over—
you, my dreaming brother,

teacher of language and thought,
gift of body and light,

miraculous in full on glory.

For Andres and Eleanor

Love heals from the inside.

Yusef Komunyakaa

Last night I left the back door open
and let the moon's breeze come over me,

and yes, I could hear you Eleanor.
I could hear you whisper Andres' name

into the darkening sky and call out
the ice worker and all of his songs.

This morning, when the moon was still there
begging for one more song, I crawled out

of bed and thought of you again. I wish
Andres, that there would be one more hour

at the café. I wish
God might declare it all a joke, but

I know how much he wanted you and
how much you wanted him, too. This is what counts.

So I'll leave you alone. I'll go now
to the sun and imagine the actions of

angels, sweetened from the sun,
whispering to the moon about revolution.

After Kundera

I choose weight—the dense exhaust of Lima
wrapping us closer as God would have it.

Beethoven says better to choose
what we can bear. While youth collect flowers, play war,

they mirage, die and forget. But the weight

bearers remember. And death is not
even the greatest weight. It is

the illogical death of your love. It will cripple you.
The light in the room illuminates the heavy sadness.

Darkness grows tired of everyone.
So flash your awkward smile to her

with a rose extended. Give her

the weight of your heart and carry the weight of hers,
all its rhythms,
all its scars,
all its perfect questions.

Casa de la Santa Lucia

Antigua, Guatemala

A white steeple rises from the tile roof
near the lime green one a little shorter
as stone streets divide mustard yellow
and tomato red store fronts, the owners
leaning against the open wall, peering
every so often down the narrow sidewalk
sprinkled with locals with bolsas on their
heads and foreigners from the language
school improving their accent
as the birds, in different voices, say
please do not forget this beauty.
We ache from such sweetness.

Hotel Posada Belen

Chichicastenango, Guatemala

Across the one lane cobbled avenue
I can see into the cement yard of a woman
whose daughter squats, pulls up her wrap,
and urinates onto the pavement
near a drain. In the distance,
near the Church of Santo Thomas probably,
another half-stick of dynamite alerts
the languid village, the cofrades are coming.
Humanity is the sloped hills tattered
with aluminum roofs, occassional smoke
from a preparation, and another
ownerless dog in mid-flight to nowhere.

Rurrenebaque

for Polly

Once, I walked
into a brown field
full of anacondas
no one could see.
In the distance
by the tree
we used as our marker
back to the boat
there were horses
easing into the evening
swishing the last of the grass
in their mouths.

In the pampas,
our long white sleeves
saved us from what
we could not name:
the indigenous facial
expressions of dreams
and heirlooms, piranha
teeth strung from a wire.

And you, stomping along
through this muddy earth,
your camera like an artifact,
your husband watching
you. In this field,

you appear in my dream:
mud-caked, sweating
from the world,
beautiful as a raindrop
from heaven.

Oaxaca City

In the old city square, where the man
sings *Oaxaca, Oaxaca, Oaxaca*,

roses are tossed from a balcony.
Of course the scene was beautiful

(sunset, southern Mexico and roses),
but this is not about beauty.

He admires the roses but wants
the seeds, money and the belief

you will buy one of his tapes, listen
when you return to the hotel, fall

into deeper love. I only remember
one woman's face—the old woman

whose cheeks were like puffy brown
clouds. Wreathed in red scarves, she sells

her wooden spoons with the city's name
burned into the handle, to remind you

how the sun shone down on her hair,
how her eyes were watching, almost

burning those rose petals into the grass.

Ghosts

They sleep with a talisman, sometimes an animal
to root themselves to the earth. They sing about mud

spread around their ancestors' faces to prompt good dreams,
the red to suggest a healthy dinner kill, the blue

for a long rain when they need it. They pray hard,
sleep harder than you think. Once, far

from here, I saw the man whose body helped birth mine.
He floated around the small room, asleep.

His talisman was fresh lizard skin wrapped tightly around
a bluejay's skeleton. He gave it a smile for hope. Around

his neck, a photograph encased in a locket, a dream
in time for the little boy's chubby face and his

stunned look of arrival, removal. Which is more
shocking? Exiting the womb of the mother,

leaving that mother forever, or leaving mother earth
entirely? Perhaps none of these? The poet should know

nothing is shocking until you meet another mother.
Then, the ghost disappeared, his face paint blueing

with the sky. Eventually, I want to float upward
slowly, imagine myself a frameless collage of

beautiful mothers, birth, life, earth, circular,
finally whole because the circle is infinite, immaculate,

indefinitely breathing love in, love out, love in.

Ghost in a Museum

The ghost of Carlos Baca Flor sighs
near the tall arches, the climbing windows stained
centuries ago, literally ages—Bronze, Middle,

Stone. And the woman at the café counter
sighs, reads Monday's news of Peru. A young boy
sweeps. Hardly any dust here. And there,
over by the window,
a woman thinks.

What dreams did Manuel Ortega have
the night he finished a painting? In my daydream,
the ghost of Carlos Baca Flor stands
near the tall arches.

Do you go to a museum to fall in love, to fall
in new love again, to forget, or to float?
Yes, it is like floating, being in a museum—
the texture of Uncle Ho's shirt,
the Lilies.

What would Vincent Van Gogh say to Ho Chi Minh
over coffee in Hue?
Would Van Gogh know more about tanks
than Uncle Ho would of flowers?

And whose self-portraits are most accurate,
the blind or the mad?

What kind of stories will your home tell,
the verandas keep,
those birds rehash into the wind?

What Is Sacred

I have no idea what priests
dream of on Christmas Eve, what prayer

a crippled dog might whine before the shotgun.
I have no more sense of what is sacred

than a monk might have, sweeping the temple
floor, slow gestures of honor to the left,

the right. Maybe the leaf of grass tells us
what is worthwhile. Maybe it tells us nothing.

Perhaps a sacred moment is a photograph
you look at over and over again, the one

of you and her, hands lightly clasped like you
did before prayer became necessary, the one

with the sinking cathedral in Mexico City rising up
behind you and a limping man frozen in time

to the right of you, the moment when she touched
your bare arm for the first time, her fingers

like cool flashes of heaven.

Lee Herrick was born in Seoul, South Korea and adopted at eleven months. His poems have appeared in the *Haight Ashbury Literary Journal*, *Berkeley Poetry Review*, *Hawaii Pacific Review*, *The Bloomsbury Review*, *Quercus Review*, *MiPOesias*, and *Many Mountains Moving*, among others, and in anthologies such as *Seeds from a Silent Tree: An Anthology of Korean Adoptees*, *Hurricane Blues: Poems About Katrina and Rita*, and *Highway 99: A Literary Journey through California's Great Central Valley*, 2nd edition. He is the founding editor of the literary magazine *In the Grove* and has been nominated for a Pushcart Prize. He is a Professor of English at Fresno City College and lives in Fresno, California.

Printed in the United States
125731LV00004B/466-513/A